YEZIDI HOLY BOOKS

YEZIDI
HOLY BOOKS

EDITED WITH AN INTRODUCTION BY
GREGORY K. KOON

ISBN-13: 978-1539162797
ISBN-10: 1539162796

CONTENTS

INTRODUCTION

The Yezidi texts compiled in this work are derived from five sources: 1) *The Nestorians and Their Rituals,* 1852, by George Percy Badger; 2) *Discoveries Among the Ruins of Nineveh and Babylon,* 1853, by Henry Layard; 3) *Six Months in a Syrian Monastery,* 1895, by Oswald Parry; 4) "Yezidi Texts", *The American Journal of Semitic Languages and Literatures,* Vol. 25, No. 3, 1909, by Isya Joseph; and 5) "Notes on the Yezidis", *The Journal of the Royal Anthropological Institute of Great Britain and Ireland* Vol. 41, 1911 by W. B. Heard.

Our first two sources, Badger and Layard, each supply us with their own version of *The Hymn of Sheikh Adi.* As recounted in his *Nestorians,* Badger's translation is from an Arabic copy which he procured "after much trouble" from a Yezidi Sheikh at Mount Lalish. Layard similarly received his version of the *Hymn* in manuscript form at Lalish, but from a Yezidi *Kawwal* named Yusuf.

Oswald Parry, our third contributor, obtained a manuscript from a native of Mosul which contained forms of both the *Al-Jilwah* and the *Mashaf Resh,* but his material lacked a copy of the *Hymn of Sheikh Adi.* He had his manuscript translated by E. G. Browne, which is the translation used here and published in Parry's *Six Months in a Syrian Monastery.* Parry's is the first edition of the *Jilwah* and *Resh* in English.

The most complete form of the Holy Texts which have been utilized for this edition are those translated from the Arabic manuscript of Daud-as-Saig (a resident of Mosul on friendly terms with some Yezidis) by our fourth source, Isya Joseph. His materials contained versions of all three of the texts featured here (*Jilwah*, *Resh*, and *Hymn*), and the copy of *Mashaf Resh* in his manuscript is much different than the one translated by Browne.

Our fifth and final source, W.B. Heard, supplies us only with our third version of *Jilwah*. The author states that the work was written "in Kurdish using Arabic characters on gazelle-skin," and that it was translated by "a Chaldean Ecclesiastic of Mosul."

The purpose of this small book is not to present a history of the Yezidis or a description of their beliefs and customs. Instead it is designed to be a simple comparison of some translations of Yezidi sacred writing.

For an in-depth analysis of the Yezidi belief system and a fuller history of the various manuscripts from which our information arises, the editor recommends *The Religion of the Yezidis*, 1930, by Giuseppe Furlani and Y*ezidism: Its Background, Observances and Textual Tradition*, 1995, by Philip G. Kreyenbroek.

NOTE:

In the present volume, all three versions of *Al-Jilwah* have been divided into verses. These were not presented in such a form in our source materials. The reason for this addition is to facilitate the side-by-side comparison of the differences in each translation. The number of verses in each chapter was decided upon by the editor and is not derived from any previous convention.

YEZIDI PRAYER

Amen, Amen, Amen!
Through the intermediation of Shams-ad-Din,
Fakhr ad-Din, Nasir-ad-Din,
Sajad ad-Din, Sheikh Sin,
Sheikh Bakr, Kadir ar-Rahman.
Lord, thou art gracious, thou art merciful;
Thou art God, king of kings and lands,
King of joy and happiness,
King of eternal life.
From eternity thou art eternal.
Thou art the seat of happiness and life;
Thou art lord of grace and good luck.
Thou art king of jinns and human beings,
King of the holy men,
Lord of terror and praise,
The abode of religious duty and praise,
Worthy of praise and thanks.
Lord! Protector in journeys,
Sovereign of the moon and of the darkness,
God of the sun and of the fire,
God of the great throne,
Lord of goodness.
Lord! No one knows how thou art.
Thou hast no beauty; thou hast no height.
Thou hast no going forth; thou hast no number.
Lord! Judge of kings and beggars,
Judge of society and of the world,
Thou hast revealed the repentance of Adam.
Lord, thou hast no house; thou hast no money;
Thou hast no wings, hast no feathers;
Thou hast no voice, thou hast no color.
Thou hast made us lucky and satisfied.
Thou hast created Jesus and Mary.
Lord, thou art gracious,
Merciful, faithful.
Thou art Lord; I am nothingness.
I am a fallen sinner,
A sinner by thee remembered.
Thou hast led us out of darkness into light.
Lord! My sin and my guilt,
Take them and remove them.
O God, O God, O God, Amen!

KITAB AL-JILWAH
THE BOOK OF REVELATION

Before all creation this revelation was with Melek Ta'us, who sent 'Abd Ta'us to this world that he might separate truth known to his particular people. This was done, first of all, by means of oral tradition, and afterward by means of this book, Al-Jilwah, which the outsiders may neither read nor behold.

Al-Jilwah is said to have been written in 1162 A. D., by Sheikh Fakhr-ad-Din, the secretary of Sheikh 'Adi, at the dictation of the latter. The original copy, wrapped in linen and silk wrappings, is kept in the house of Mulla Haidar, of Baadrie. Twice a year the book is taken to Sheikh 'Adi's shrine. - *Isya Joseph*

CHAPTER I

1. I was, and am now, and will continue unto eternity, ruling over all creatures and ordering the affairs and deeds of those who are under my sway.

2. I am presently at hand to such as trust in me and call upon me in time of need, neither is there any place void of me where I am not present.

3. I am thine evil in all those events which strangers name evils because they are not done according to their desire.

4. Every age has a Regent, and this by my counsel. Every generation changes with the Chief of this World, so that each one of the chiefs in his turn and cycle fulfils his charge.

5. I grant indulgence according to the just merits of those qualities wherewith each disposition is by nature endowed.

6. He who opposeth me vexeth and grieveth the other gods, to whom it is not given to interfere in my business and work: whatsoever I determine, that is.

7. The Scriptures which are in the hands of strangers, even though they were written by prophets and apostles, yet have these turned aside, and rebelled, and perverted them; and each one of them confuteth the other and abrogateth it.

8. Truth and Falsehood are distinguished by proving them at the time of their appearance.

9. I will fulfill my promise to those who put their trust in me,

10. And will perform my covenant, or will act contrary to it, according to the judgment of those wise and discerning Regents to whom I have delegated my authority for determinate periods.

11. I take note of all affairs, and promote the performance of what is needful in its due time.

12. I direct and teach such as will follow my teaching, who find in their accord with me joy and delight greater than any joy wherewith the soul rejoiceth.

CHAPTER II

1. I reward and I punish this progeny of Adam in all different ways of which I have knowledge.

2. In this my hand is the control of the earth and what is above it and beneath it.

3. I undertake not the assistance of other races,

4. Neither do I withhold good from them; much less do I [grudge it] to those who are my chosen people and obedient servants. I surrender active control into the hands of those whom I have proved, who are, in accordance with my will, friends in some shape and fashion to such as are faithful and abide by my counsel.

5. I take and I give; I make rich and I make poor; I make happy and I make wretched, according to environments and seasons,

6. And there is none who hath the right to interfere, or to withdraw any man from my control. I draw down

pains and sicknesses upon such as strive to thwart me. He who is accounted mine, dieth not like other men.

7. I suffer no man to dwell in this lower world for more than the period determined by me; and, if I wish, I send him back into this world a second and a third time, or more, by the transmigration of the soul, and this by a universal law.

CHAPTER III

1. I guide without a revealed book; I point the way by unseen means unto my friends and such as observe the precepts of my teaching, which is not grievous, and is adapted to the time and conditions.

2. I punish such as contravene my laws in other worlds.

3. The children of this Adam know not those things which are determined, wherefore they oft-times fall into error.

4. The beasts of the field, and of heaven, and the fish of the sea, all of them are in my hand and under my control.

5. The treasures and hoards buried in the heart of the earth are known to me, and I cause one after another to inherit them.

6. I make manifest my signs and wonders to such as will receive them and seek them from me in their due season. The antagonism and opposition of strangers to me and my followers do but injure the authors thereof, because they know not that might and wealth are in my hands, and that I bestow them on such of Adam's progeny as are deserving of them.

7.The ordering of the worlds, the revolution of ages, and the changing of their regents are mine from eternity. And whosoever walketh not uprightly therein, him will I chastise in my own appointed time, and turn back to his former charge.

CHAPTER IV

1. The seasons are four, and the elements are four; these have I vouchsafed to meet the needs of my creatures.

2. The scriptures of strangers are accepted by me in so far as they accord and agree with my ordinances and run not counter to them; for they have been for the most part perverted.

3. Three there are opposed to me, and three names do I hate.

4. To such as keep my secrets shall my promises be fulfilled.

5. All those who have under-gone tribulations for my sake, will I recompense without fail in one of the worlds.

6. I desire all my followers to be united in one fold on account of those who are antagonists and strangers to them.

7. 0 ye who observe my injunctions, reject such sayings and teachings as are not from me.

8. Mention not my name or my attributes, as strangers do, lest ye be guilty of sin, for ye have no knowledge thereof.

CHAPTER V

1. Honour my symbol and image, for it will remind you of what ye have neglected of my laws and ordinances.

2. Be obedient to my servants and act with sincerity towards them, in gratitude for what they communicate to you of that knowledge of the unseen which they receive from me.

CHAPTER I

1. I was, am now, and shall have no end. I exercise dominion over all creatures and over the affairs of all who are under the protection of my image.

2. I am ever present to help all who trust in me and call upon me in time of need. There is no place in the universe that knows not my presence.

3. I participate in all the affairs which those who are without call evil because their nature is not such as they approve.

4. Every age has its own manager, who directs affairs according to my decrees. This office is changeable from generation to generation, that the ruler of this world and his chiefs may discharge the duties of their respective offices every one in his own turn.

5. I allow everyone to follow the dictates of his own nature,

6. But he that opposes me will regret it sorely. No god has a right to interfere in my affairs, and I have made it an imperative rule that everyone shall refrain from worshiping all gods.

7. All the books of those who are without are altered by them; and they have declined from them, although they were written by the prophets and the apostles. That there are interpolations is seen in the fact that each sect endeavors to prove that the others are wrong and to destroy their books.

8. To me truth and falsehood are known.

9. When temptation comes, I give my covenant to him that trusts in me.

10. Moreover, I give counsel to the skilled directors, for I have appointed them for periods that are known to me.

11. I remember necessary affairs and execute them in due time.

12. I teach and guide those who follow my instruction. If anyone obey me and conform to my commandments, he shall have joy, delight, and goodness.

CHAPTER II

1. I requite the descendents of Adam, and reward them with various rewards that I alone know.

2. Moreover, power and dominion over all that is on earth, both that which is above and that which is beneath, are in my hand.

3. I do not allow friendly association with other people,

4. Nor do I deprive them that are my own and that obey me of anything that is good for them. I place my affairs in the hands of those whom I have tried and who are in accord with my desires. I appear in divers manners to those who are faithful and under my command.

5. I give and take away; I enrich and impoverish; I cause both happiness and misery. I do all this in keeping with the characteristics of each epoch.

6. And none has a right to interfere with my management of affairs. Those who oppose me I afflict with disease; but my own shall not die like the sons of Adam that are without.

7. None shall live in this world longer than the time set by me; and if I so desire, I send a person a second or a third time into this world or into some other by the transmigration of souls.

CHAPTER III

1. I lead to the straight path without a revealed book; I direct aright my beloved and my chosen ones by unseen means. All my teachings are easily applicable to all times and all conditions.

2. I punish in another world all who do contrary to my will.

3. Now the sons of Adam do not know the state of things that is to come. For this reason they fall into many errors.

4. The beasts of the earth, the birds of heaven, and the fish of the sea are all under the control of my hands.

5. All treasures and hidden things are known to me; and as I desire, I take them from one and bestow them upon another.

6. I reveal my wonders to those who seek them, and, in due time my miracles to those who receive them from me. But those who are without are my adversaries, hence they oppose me. Nor do they know that such a course is against their own interests, for might, wealth, and riches are in my hand, and I bestow them upon every worthy descendant of Adam.

7. Thus the government of the worlds, the transition of generations, and the changes of their directors are determined by me from the beginning.

1. I will not give my rights to other gods. I have allowed the creation of four substances, four times, and four corners; because they are necessary things for creatures.

2. The books of Jews, Christians, and Moslems, as of those who are without, accept in a sense, i.e., so far as they agree with, and conform to, my statutes. Whatsoever is contrary to these they have altered; do not accept it.

3. Three things are against me, and I hate three things.

4. But those who keep my secrets shall receive the fulfillment of my promises.

5. Those who suffer for my sake I will surely reward in one of the worlds.

6. It is my desire that all my followers shall unite in a bond of unity, lest those who are without prevail against them.

7. Now, then, all ye who have followed my commandments and my teachings, reject all the teachings and sayings of such as are without. I have not taught these teachings, nor do they proceed from me.

8. Do not mention my name nor my attributes, lest ye regret it; for ye do not know what those who are without may do.

CHAPTER V

1. O ye that have believed in me, honor my symbol and my image, for they remind you of me.

2. Observe my laws and statutes. Obey my servants and listen to whatever they may dictate to you of the hidden things. Receive that that is dictated, and do not carry it before those who are without, Jews, Christians, Moslems, and others; for they know not the nature of my teaching. Do not give them your books, lest they alter them without your knowledge. Learn by heart the greater part of them, lest they be altered.

CHAPTER I

1. I was, I am present now and shall remain until the end. I rule over all creatures. I ordain the works and affairs of all men existing under my powerful hand.

2. When and where it is needful, I am ready to help all that ask, search and call for me. I am present everywhere; there is no place where I cannot be found.

3. All evil that exists or happens to mankind, I am therein, and it happens with my knowledge; and because evil happens against the will of men, so they call it evil.

4. Every period has its special order, and that through my knowledge. Each period has its ruler (*hukindar*), and at the end of each period a new one succeeds him.

5. I allow all creatures to make or burn (destroy?) according to their habit and taste.

6. Any man who works against me will repent and be ashamed. Other Gods cannot interfere with my work, and what I wish to do, they cannot prevent it.

7. All books which are in the hands of those outside my religion, though written by prophets and apostles, are crooked and pervert the truth. The latest book (Jelwet) cancels all others.

8. You may understand what is true or false by trying it.

9. I fulfill my promise to him who trusts us.

10. I am free to fulfill or not my promise according to the information given to me by those whom I have ordained to rule the periods and guide my people.

11. The needful orders and work at the time I mention and fulfill.

12. I teach my law to those who obey me, and they will have peace and success as long as they keep peace with me.

CHAPTER II

1. I punish the race of Adam, and reward whom I will.

2. I reign over the earth, and over the height and depth.

3. I allow no man to work against me.

4. I do not forbid good to those who obey and believe me. I reveal myself in different ways to those who follow and hear me.

5. I give and I take. I make rich and poor. I make fortunate and unfortunate. I give prosperity and misfortune.

6. Those who are under my power cannot interfere with my work or forbid me; though they are against me I give them sickness and trouble.

7. I allow no man to live longer than I have ordained, and when I will, the second and third time I raise him alive again.

CHAPTER III

1. I lead the people without books, and bring them to the right way. My laws are not heavy to bear, they are suited to the time and circumstances.

2. And whoso worketh against my judgment, I punish him.

3. The children of Adam do err because they cannot comprehend the future.

4. All the beasts of the desert and the birds of the air and the fishes of the sea, all are under my hand and power.

5. All the mines of the heart of the earth are evident to me, and I transfer from one to the other.

6. My power and miracles I show to those who ask me, and all who work against me shall be troubled because they do not know that riches and poverty are in my hand, and I give to the children of Adam who deserve.

7. Since the beginning, the succession of men, periods and nations, and the change of rulers I have ordained.

CHAPTER IV

1. My rights I give to no other God. I have created four elements of the earth to fulfill the needs of men, which are water, earth, wind and fire. And I have created the four seasons of the year and the four foundations of the earth.

2. I accept the sacred books of other nations, so long as they agree with my laws.

3. Three things are against me, and three names I hate.

4. He who fulfills my mysteries shall enjoy my promises.

5. I will reward him who suffers for me.

6. I desire that all my subjects be united, and that they should oppose other nations.

7. Oh! ye my people who hear my voice, deny everything and every word which does not come forth from me.

8. Ye must not utter my name, nor speak of my shape, for if ye do it is a sin. Ye must not be careless like other nations for this.

CHAPTER V

1. Respect my image and myself, for when ye leave the path of my truth, they will lead ye aright.

2. Obey my servants. Hear and perfect the knowledge and mysteries they make known to you from them.

، كِتَاب ٱلجَلْوَة ،

الموجود قبل كل الخلايف عند طاوس ملك وهو ارسل الى هذا العالم عبد طاوس لكي يميِّز ويفهِّم ويعلم لشعبهِ الخاص من التيه اولاً بتسليم مشافهة وثم بهذا كتاب الجلوة الذي ما يجوز لاحد من الخارجين ان يقراهُ او يراهُ.

، الفصل الاول ،

انا كنت. وموجود الان. وليس لي نهاية. ولي تسلط على الخلايف. وتدبير مصالح كل الذين تحت صورتي. وانا حاضراً سريعًا للذين يثقون بي ويدعوني وقت الحاجة. ما يخلو عني مكان من الدنيا. مشترك انا بجميع وقايع التي يسمونها الخارجين شرو، لانها ليست حسب مرامهم. كل زمن لهُ مدبِّر وذلك بشَوري. كل جيل يتغير. حتى رئس هذا العالم والروسآء يكون كل واحد بدورهِ ونوبتهِ لكي يكمِّل وظيفتهُ. اعطى رخصة حسب حق الطبيعة للانسان. يندم ويحـزن الذي يقاومني جميع الالهة ليس لهـم مداخلة بشغلي ومنعي عنهما قضيّة مهمَّة كانت جميع الكـتـب الموجودة بيـن الخارجين بدّلوا فيها وزاغوا عـنـهـا ولو كتبوها الانبياء والمرسلين لان كل واحد يبطل الآخر وينسخ كتابهُ. الحق والبطل معلوم عندي. حين وقوعهم مـن التجربة اعطي ميثاقي للذين يتكلون عليَّ واعطيهم راي المديرين الحذّاق لاني وكلتهم لاوقات معلومة عندي. اذكر واحرك امور اللازمة في حينها. ارشد واعلم الذين يتبعون تعليمي. واذا سمعوا قولي ووافقوا مـشـورتـي يجدون فيهِ لذةً وفرحًا وخيرًا لهم.

الفصل الثاني ٠

انا اكني واجازي نسل آدم بانواع اعرفها. بيدي قوى وتسلط على جميع ما في الارض من فوقها وتحتها. ما اقبل مصادقة غير عوالم. وما امنع خير الذين مم خاصتي وبطوعي. اسلم شغلي بيد الذين جربتهم ومم حسب مرامي. اظهر ببعض الانواع والاشكال للذين مم أمينين وتحت شوري. احذ واعطي. اغني وافقر. اسعد واشقي. وذلك حسب الظروف والاوقات وليس مـن يحـف لـهُ ان يتداخل بشي من تصرفي. اجلب الارجاع على الذين يضادّدوني ما يموت الذي هو من حسبي مثل الخارجين من بني ادم. ما اسمح لاحد بان يسكن هذه الدنيا اكثر مـن الزمن الحـدود مني. واذا شِئتُ ارسلتهُ مرة اخرى ثانيًا وثالثًا الى هذا العالم او الى غيره بتناسخ الارواح.

الفصل الثالث ٠

ارشد من غير كتاب. اهدي غيبًا احباي وخواصي. جـمـيـع تعالمبي بلا كلفة موافقة للحال والزمان. اقاصص الذين يخالفون شرايعي بعوالم الاخر. بنوا هذا ادم ما يعرفون الاحوال المزمعة لذلك يسقطون اوقات كـثيرة بغلط. حيوانات البر وطيور السماء وسمك البحر جميعهم بيدي وتحت ضبطي. جميع الخزاين والدفاين التي تحت الارض عندي واخلفها من واحد الى واحد لمن اريدهُ. اظهر مجِزاتي وعجايبي للذين يقبلوها ويطلبوها مني في حينها. والاجنبيين مم مخالفون ومضاددون لي ولا يبالون بذلك ومم مـا يدرون هـي ضرر عليهم. لان العظمة والثروة والغنى مم بـيـدي.

وانا اختار من يليق لها من نسل آدم. وتدابير العوالم وانقلاب الاجيال وتغير مديرينهم منظومة مني منذ القديم.

.. الفصل الرابع ..

حقوقي ما اعطيها لغيري مـن الالهة. اربعة عناصر. واربـعـة ازمنة. واربعة اركان سخت بها لاجل ضروريات المخلوقين. كتب الاجانب من اليهود والنصارى والاسلام اقبلوا مـنـهـا ما يوافق ويطابق سنني. وما يخالف منها فلا تقبلوهُ لانهم غيّروهُ. ثـلـث اشيـاء هي ضدي وثلث اشياء ابغضها. الذين يحفظون اسراري ينالون مواعيدي. والذين ينالون المصايب بـسـبـبـي لابد ان اكافيهم باحد العوالم. جميع تابعيَّ اريد ان يتحدوا برباط واحد لئلا يضادهم الاجانب. يا ايها الذين تبعتم كل وصاياى وتعاليمى انكروا كل تعاليم واقوال الاجانب التي ليست انا علمتها وليست هي من عندي. لا تذكرون اسمي ولا صفاتي لئلا تندبون لانكم لستم تدرون ما يفعلون الاجانب.

.. الفصل الخامس ..

يا ايها الذين امنوا اكـرموا شخصي وصررتي لانهم يذكرونكم بي. احفظوا سنني وشرايعي. طيعوا واصغوا لخدامي بما يلقنوكم من علم الغيب الذي هو من عندي. احتفظوا بالعلم الذي يلقنوكـم اياه ولا تحبوا بهِ قدام الاجانب كاليهود والنصارى والاسلام وغيرهم. لانهم لا يدرون ما هو تعليمي ولا تعطوهم من كتبكم لئلاً يغيروها عليكم وانتم لا تعلمون. احفظوا احفظوا اكثر الاشياء غيبًا لئلا تتغير عليكم.

The Hymn of Sheikh Adi

Peace Be Upon Him

1. My wisdom knoweth the truth of things,

2. And my truth hath mingled with me.

3. My real descent is from myself;

4. I have not known evil to be with me.

5. All creation is under my control;

6. Through me are the habitable parts and the deserts,

7. And every created thing is subservient to me.

8. And I am he that decreeth and causeth existence.

9. I am he that spake the true word,

10. And I am he that dispenseth power, and I am the ruler of the earth.

11. And I am he that guideth mankind to worship my majesty.

12. And they came unto me and kissed my feet.

13. And I am he that pervadeth the highest heavens;

14, And I am he that cried in the wilderness;

15. And I am the Sheikh, the one, the only one;

16. And I am he that by myself revealeth things;

17. And I am he to whom the book of glad tidings came down

18. From my Lord who cleaveth the mountains.

19. And I am he to whom all men came,

20. Obedient to me they kissed my feet.

21. I am the mouth, the moisture of whose spittle

22. Is as honey, wherewith I constitute my confidants.

23. And by his light he hath lighted the lamp of the morning.

24. I guide him that seeketh my direction.

25. And I am he that placed Adam in my paradise.

26. And I am he that made Nimrod a hot burning fire.

27. And I am he that guided Ahmet mine elect,

28. I gifted him with my way and guidance.

29. Mine are all existences together,

30. They are my gift and under my direction.

31. And I am he that possesseth all majesty.

32. And beneficence and charity are from my grace.

33. And I am he that entereth the heart in my zeal;

34. And I shine through the power of my awfulness and majesty.

35. And I am he to whom the lion of the desert came,

36. I rebuked him and he became like stone.

37. And I am he to whom the serpent came,

38. And by my will I made him like dust.

39. And I am he that shook the rock and made it tremble,

40. And sweet water flowed therefrom on every side.

41. And I am he that brought down an authentic verity,—

42. A book whereby I will guide the prudent ones.

43. And I am he that enacted a powerful law.

44. And its promulgation was my gift.

45. And I am he that brought from the fountain water

46. Limpid and sweeter than all waters;

47. And I am he that disclosed it in my mercy.

48. And in my might I called it the white fountain.

49. And I am he to whom the Lord of heaven said:

50. Thou art the ruler and governor of the universe.

51. And I am he who manifested some of my wonders,

52. And some of my virtues are seen in the things that exist.

53. And I am he to whom the flinty mountains bow,

54. They are under me, and ask to do my pleasure.

55. And I am he before whose majesty the wild beasts wept;

56. They came and worshipped and kissed my feet.

57. I am Adi of the mark, a wanderer,—

58. The All-Merciful has distinguished me with names.

59. And my seat and throne are the wide-spread earth.

60. In the depth of my knowledge there is no God but me.

61. These things are subservient to my power.

62. How, then, can ye deny me, O mine enemies?

63. Do not deny me, O men, but yield,

64. That in the day of the resurrection you may be happy in meeting with me.

65. He who dies enraptured with me, I will cast him

66. In the midst of paradise, after my pleasure, and by my will;

67. But he who dies neglectful of me

68. Shall be punished with my contempt and rod.

69. And I declare that I am the essential one:

70. I create and provide for those who do my will.

71. Praise be to mine essence; for all things are by my will.

72. And the world is lighted with some of my gifts.

73. I am the great and majestic king;

74. It is I who provide for the wants of men.

75. I have made known to you, O congregation, some of my ways.

76. Who desireth me must forsake the world.

77. I am he that spake a true word;

78. The highest heavens are for those who obey me.

79. I sought out truth, and became the establisher of truth;

80. And with a similar truth shall they attain to the highest like me.

1. My understanding surrounds the truth of things,

2. And my truth is mixed up in me.

3. And the truth of my descent is set forth by itself.

4. And when it was known it was altogether in me.

5. All who are in the universe are under me,

6. And all the habitable parts and the deserts,

7. And every thing created is under me.

8. And I am the ruling power preceding all that exists.

9. And I am he who spake a true saying.

10. And I am the just judge, and the ruler of the earth.

11. And I am he whom men worship in my glory,

12. Coming to me and kissing my feet.

13. And I am he who spread over the heavens their height.

14. And I am he who cried in the beginning (or in the wilderness, *Al bidaee*).

15. And I am the Sheikh, the one and only one.

16. And I am he who of myself revealeth all things.

17. And I am he to whom came the book of glad tidings,

18. From my Lord who burneth the mountains.

19. And I am he to whom all created men come,

20. In obedience to kiss my feet.

21. I bring forth fruit from the first juice of early youth,

22. By my presence, and turn towards me my disciples.

23. And before his light the darkness of the morning cleared away.

24. I guide him who asketh for guidance.

25. And I am he that caused Adam to dwell in Paradise,

26. And Nimrod to inhabit a hot burning fire.

27. And I am he who guided Ahmed the Just,

28. And led him into my path and way.

29. And I am he unto whom all creatures

30. Come unto for my good purposes and gifts.

31. And I am he who visited all the heights,

32. And goodness and charity proceed from my mercy.

33. And I am he who made all hearts to fear

34. My purpose, and they magnified the power and majesty of my awfulness.

35. And I am he to whom the destroying lion came,

36. Raging, and I shouted against him and he became stone.

37. And I am he to whom the serpent came,

38. And by my will I made him dust.

39. And I am he who struck the rock and made it tremble,

40. And made to burst from its side the sweetest of waters.

41. And I am he who sent down the certain truth.

42. From me is the book that comforteth the oppressed.

43. And I am he who judged justly;

44. And when I judged it was my right.

45. And I am he who made the springs to give water,

46. Sweeter and pleasanter than all waters.

47. And I am he that caused it to appear in my mercy,

48. And by my power I called it the pure.

49. And I am he to whom the Lord of Heaven hath said,

50. Thou art the Just Judge, and the ruler of the earth.

51. And I am he who disclosed some of my wonders.

52. And some of my virtues are manifested in that which exists.

53. And I am he who caused the mountains to bow,

54. To move under me, and at my will.

55. And I am he before whose awful majesty the wild beasts cried;

56. They turned to me worshipping, and kissed my feet.

57. And I am Adi Es-shami (or, of Damascus), the son of Moosafir.

58. Verily the All-Merciful has assigned unto me names,

59. The heavenly throne, and the seat, and the seven heavens and the earth.

60. In the secret of my knowledge there is no God but me.

61. These things are subservient to my power.

62. And for which state do you deny my guidance.

63. Oh men ! deny me not, but submit;

64. In the day of Judgment you will be happy in meeting me.

65. Who dies in my love I will cast him

66. In the midst of Paradise by my will and pleasure;

67. But he who dies unmindful of me,

68. Will be thrown into torture in misery and affliction.

69. I say that I am the only one and the exalted;

70. I create and make rich those whom I will.

71. Praise be to myself, and all things are by my will

72. And the universe is lighted by some of my gifts.

73. I am the King who magnifies himself;

74. And all the riches of creation are at my bidding.

75. I have made known unto you, O people, some of my ways,

76. Who desireth me must forsake the world.

77. And I can also speak the true saying.

78. And the garden on high is for those who do my pleasure.

79. I sought the truth, and became a confirming truth;

80. And by the like truth shall they possess the highest place like me.

1. My understanding surrounds the truth of things,

2. And my truth is mixed up in me,

3. And the truth of my descent is set forth by itself,

4. And when it was known it was altogether in me.

5. And all that are in the universe are under me,

6. And all the habitable parts and deserts,

7. And everything created is under me,

8. And I am the ruling power preceding all that exists.

9. And I am he that spoke a true saying,

10. And I am the just judge and the ruler of the earth.

11. And I am he that men worship in my glory,

12. Coming to me and kissing my feet.

13. And I am he that spread over the heavens their height.

14. And I am he that cried in the beginning.

15. And I am he that of myself revealeth all things,

16. And I am he to whom came the book of good tidings

17. From my Lord, who burneth the mountains.

18. And I am he to whom all created men come

19. In obedience to kiss my feet.

20. I bring forth fruit from the first juice of early youth

21. By my presence, and turn toward me my disciples.

22. And before this light the darkness of the morning cleared away.

23. I guide him that asketh for guidance.

24. I am he that caused Adam to dwell in Paradise

25. And Nimrod to inhabit a hot burning fire.

26. And I am he that guided Ahmed the Just,

27. And let him into my path and way.

28. And I am he unto whom all creatures

29. Come for my good purposes and gifts.

30. And I am he that visited all the heights,

31. And goodness and charity proceed from my mercy.

32. And I am he that made all hearts to fear

33. My purpose, and they magnify the majesty and power of my awfulness.

34. And I am he to whom the destroying lion came

35. Raging, and I shouted against him and he became stone.

36. And I am he to whom the serpent came,

37. And by my will I made him dust.

38. And I am he that struck the rock and made it tremble,

39. And made to burst from its sides the sweetest of waters.

40. And I am he that sent down the certain truth;

41. For me is the book that comforteth the oppressed.

42. And I am he that judged justly,

43. And when I judged it was my right

44. And I am he that made the springs38 to give water,

45. Sweeter and pleasanter than all waters.

46. And I am he that caused it to appear in my mercy,

47. And by my power I called it the pure.

48. And I am he to whom the Lord of heaven hath said,

49. Thou art the just Judge and Ruler of the earth.

50. And I am he that disclosed some of my wonders,

51. And some of my virtues are manifested in that which exists.

52. And I am he that caused the mountains to bow,

53. To move under me and at my will.

54. And I am he before whose majesty the wild beasts cried;

55. They turned to me worshiping, and kissed my feet.

56. And I am 'Adi as-Sami, the son of Musafir.

57. Verily the All-Merciful has assigned unto me names,

58. The heavenly throne, and the seat, and the seven heavens, and the earth.

59. In the secret of my knowledge there is no God but me.

60. These things are subservient to my power.

61. O mine enemies, why do you deny me?

62. O men, deny me not, but submit.

63. In the day of judgment you will be happy in meeting me.

64. Who dies in my love, I will cast him

65. In the midst of Paradise, by my will and pleasure;

66. But he that dies unmindful of me

67. Will be thrown into torture in misery and affliction.

68. 1 say I am the only one and the exalted;

69. I create and make rich those whom I will.

70. Praise it to myself, for all things are by my will,

71. And the universe is lighted by some of my gifts.

72. I am the king that magnifies himself,

73. And all the riches of creation are at my bidding.

74. I have made known unto you, O people, some of my ways.

75. Who desireth me must forsake the world.

76. And I can also speak the true saying,

78. And the garden on high is for those who do my pleasure.

79. I sought the truth and became a confirming truth;

80. And by the like truth shall they, like myself, possess the highest place.

« مديحة شيخ عادي »

فهمي يحيط الحقايف — وحقي مختلط فيَّ

وحق نسلي يظهر من ذاتهِ — ولما عرف كلهُ كان في

كل الذين من العالم هم تحتي — وكل المسكونة والبراري

وكل مخلوق تحتي — وانا قوة مالكة سابقة كل موجود

وانا هو الذي تكلم كلاماً حقاً — وانا الديان العادل وحاكم الارض

وانا هو الذي تعبدني الناس في مجدي — ياتوا اليَّ ويبوسوا رجليَّ

وانا الذي بسط فوق السموات علامهم — وانا الذي صرخ في البداية

[الاشباء]

وانا الشيخ الواحد الوحيد — وانا الذي اعلن من نفسي كل

وانا الذي اتاني كتاب البشاير — من عند ربي الذي يحرق الجبال

وانا الذي ياتون اليهِ كل الرجال المخلوقين — ليبوسوا رجليَّ بطاعةٍ

اعطي ثمراً من اول عصير الحدائة — بحضوري وارجع اليَّ تلاميذي

وقدام نورهِ ظلام الصباح زال — ارشد الذي يسأل الارشاد

وانا الذي جعل ادم ان يسكن الفردوس — ونمرود يسكن نار مشتعلة

وانا الذي قاد احمد العادل — وقادهُ الى طريقي وسبيلي

وانا الذي كل الخلايف — تاتي لاجل مقاصدي وعطاياي الجيدة

وجودة وصدقة تخرج مني	وانا الذي زار كل العلاء
مقاصدي ويعظموا قوة وعزّ رعبي	وانا الذي جعل كل القلوب تخاف
وارادتي عملتها تراب	وانا الذي اليهِ الحية اتت
وجعل احلى المياه تخرج من جانبهِ	وانا الذي ضرب العخر فارتعش
من عندي الكتاب الذي يسلي المظلوم	وانا الذي انزل بعض الحق
ولما حكمتُ كان حقي	وانا الذي حكم بعدل
احلى واللّ من كل الامطار	وانا الذي جعل العيون تعطي ماء
رحمتي وبقوتي دعوتهُ الطاهر	وانا الذي جعلهُ ان يظهر في
انت الحاكم العادل وحاكم الارض	وانا الذي لهُ قال رب السماء
وبـعـض فـضـايـلي ظـاهـرة في الموجودات	وانا الذي اعـلـن بـعـض من عجايبي
تنزتحرك تحتي وعند ارادتي	وانا الذي جعل الجبال تحتي
رجعوا اليّ عابدين وقبلوا رجليّ	وانا الذي صرخت الوحوش قدام عزهِ المهيب
أن الرحمان الرحيم اعطاني اسماء والسبعة والارض	وانا عادي الشامي ابن مسافر العرش السماوي والكرسي
هذه الاشياء خادمة لقوتي	في سر معرفتني ما يوجد اله غيري
يا ناس لا تنكروني لكن اخضعوا	ويا اعداي لِمّا تنكروني
الذي يموت في حبي سالقبهِ	في ملاقاتي سيكون سعيد في يوم الدينونة
لكن من يموت غير بالي عني	في وسط الفردوس بارادتي ومسرتي

سيطرح في العذاب المصيب والشقي   اقول اني الوحيد والمتعالي

اخلق واغني من اريد   المدح لنفسي وكل الاشيـاء بارادتي هي

والكون يتنور ببعض من عطاياي   انا الملك الذي يعظم نفسهُ

وكل غناء الخليقة عند امري   عرفتكم يا شعبي بعض طرقي

من يشتاقني لازم يترك العالم   وايضاً انـا اقدر اتكلّم الـكـلام الحقيقي

والجنة في الاعالي هي للذين يعملون مـسـرتي طلبتُ الحق وصا،
حق مثبت وبكذا حق سيملكون مثلي المكان الاعلى.

47

MASHAF RESH

THE BLACK BOOK

The Black Book is said to have been written by a certain Hasan al-Basri, in 1342-1343 A. D. The original copy is kept in the house of Kehyah (chief) 'Ali, of Kasr 'Az-ad-Din, one hour west of Semale, a village east of Tigris. The book rests upon a throne, having over it a thin covering of red broadcloth, of linen, and other wrappings. Then is disclosed the binding, which is of wood. - *Isya Jospeh*

In the beginning God created the White Pearl out of His most precious Essence; and He created a bird named *Anghar*. And He placed the pearl upon its back, and dwelt thereon forty thousand years. On the first day, Sunday, He created an angel named *'Azazil*, which is *Ta'us Malak* (the Peacock Angel), the chief of all. On Monday He created *Darda'il*, which is Sheykh Hasan. On Tuesday He created *Israfil*, who is Sheykh Shams ad-Din. On Wednesday He created *Mika'il*, who is Sheykh Abu Bekr. On Thursday He created *'Azra'il*, who is Sajadin. On Friday He created the angel *Shemna'il*, who is Nasiru'd-Din. On Saturday He created the angel *Nura'il*, who is of the religion of *Malak Ta'us*; and him He made chief over them. Afterwards He created the form of the seven heavens, and the earth, and the sun, and the moon. He created mankind, and animals, and birds, and beasts, and placed them in the folds of His mantle, and arose from the Pearl, accompanied by the angels. Then He cried out at the Pearl with a loud cry, and forthwith it fell asunder into four pieces, and water gushed out from within it and became the sea. The world was round without corners. Then He created Gabriel in the form of a bird, and committed to his hands the deposition of the four corners. Then He created an ark and abode therein thirty thousand years, after which He came and dwelt in Lalesh. He cried out in the world, and the sea coagulated, and the world became worms which continued to wriggle. Then He commanded Gabriel to take two of the pieces of the White Pearl, one of which He placed under the earth, while the other rested in the Gate of Heaven. Then He placed in them the sun and the moon, and created the stars from their fragments, and suspended them in heaven for an ornament. He also created fruit-bearing trees and plants in the earth, and likewise the mountains. to embellish the earth. He created the Throne over the Carpet. Then said the Mighty Lord, "O Angels, I will create Adam and Eve, and will make them human beings, and from them two shall arise, out of the loins of Adam *Shehr ibn Jebr*; and from Adam alone shall arise a single people on the earth, the people of 'Azazil, to wit of Ta'us Malak, which is the Yezidi people." Then He sent Sheykh 'Adi b. Musafir from the land of Syria, and he came and dwelt in Lalesh. Then the Lord descended to the Holy Land, that is Jerusalem (*el-Quds*), and commanded Gabriel to take earth from the four corners of the world: earth, air, fire, and water. He made it [man], and endowed it with a soul by His power.

Then He commanded Gabriel to enter Paradise and to eat of the fruit of every green herb, only of wheat should he not eat. After a hundred years *Ta'us Malak* said to God, "How shall Adam increase and multiply, and where is his offspring?" God said to him, "Into thy hand have I surrendered authority and administration." Then He came and said to Adam, "Hast thou eaten of the wheat?" He answered, "No, for God hath forbidden me so to do, and hath said, 'Thou shalt not eat of it.'" *Malak Ta'us* said to him, "Nay, but all shall go better with thee." But, after he had eaten, his belly swelled up, and *Ta'us Malak* drove him forth from Paradise, and left him, and ascended into heaven. Then Adam suffered from the distension of his belly, because it had no outlet. But God sent a bird, which came and helped him, and made an outlet for it, and he was relieved.

And Gabriel continued absent from him for a hundred years, and he was sad, and wept. Then God commanded Gabriel, and he came and created Eve from under Adam's left arm-pit.

Then *Malak Ta'us* descended to earth for the sake of our people—I mean the much-suffering Yezidis—and raised up for us kings beside the kings of the ancient Assyrians, *Nesrukh* (who is Nasiru'd-Din), and *Kamush*. (who is King Fakhru'd-Din), and *Artimus* (who is King Shamsu'd-Din). And after this we had two kings, the first and the second Shapur, whose rule lasted one hundred and fifty years, and from whose seed are our *Amirs* until the present day; and we became divided into four Septs. To us it is forbidden to eat lettuce (*khass*)—because its name resembles that of our prophetess *Khassa*—and haricot beans; also to dye [our garments] dark blue; neither do we eat fish, out of respect for Jonah the prophet; nor gazelles, because these constituted the flock of one of our prophets. The Sheykh and his disciples, moreover, eat not the flesh of the cock, out of respect for the peacock; for it is one of the seven gods before mentioned, and its image is in the form of a cock. The Sheykh and his disciples likewise abstain from eating the flesh of hornless beasts. It is, moreover, forbidden to us to make water standing, or to put on our clothes sitting, or to cleanse ourselves in the privy as do the Muhammadans, or to perform our ablutions in their baths. Neither is it permitted to us to pronounce the name of Satan (because it is the name of our God), nor any name resembling this, such as *Kitan, Sharr, Shatt*; nor any vocable resembling *mal'un* in sound, such as *na'l*, or the like.

Before [Christ]* our religion was called idolatry; and

---

* The word "Christ" was inserted here from Joseph's version by the editor. In the original 1852 version this word was left blank, with this note by Browne:
"The text of the first part of this sentence is so corrupt that I cannot even conjecture its meaning."

the Jews, Christians, Muslims, and Persians held aloof from our religion. King Ahab and Amon were of us, so that they used to call the God of Ahab Beelzebub, whom they now call amongst us *Pir-bub*. We had a king in Babel whose name was Bukhti-Nossor (Nebuchadnezzar), and Ahasuerus in Persia, and in Constantinople Agricola.

Before heaven and earth existed, God was over the waters in an ark in the midst of the waters. Then He was wroth with the pearl which he had created, wherefore he cast it away; and from the crash of it were produced the mountains, and from the clang of it the sand-hills, and from its smoke the heavens. Then God ascended into heaven, and condensed the heavens, and fixed them in their place without supports, and enclosed the earth. Then He took the pen in His hands, and began to write down the names of all His creatures.

From His essence and light He created six gods, whose creation was as one lighteth a lamp from another lamp. Then said the first god to the second god. "I have created heaven; ascend thou into it, and create something else." And when he ascended, the sun came into being. And he said to the next, "Ascend!" and the moon came into being. And the third put the heavens in movement, and the fourth created the stars, and the fifth created *el-Kuragh*— that is to say, the Morning Star; and so on.

In the beginning God created the White Pearl out of his most precious essence. He also created a bird named Angar. He placed the White Pearl on the back of the bird, and dwelt on it for forty thousand years. On the first day, Sunday, God created Melek Azazil, and he is Ta'us-Melek, the chief of all. On Monday he created Melek Dardael, and he is Sheikh Hasan. Tuesday he created Melek Israfel, and he is Sheikh Shams (ad-Din). Wednesday he created Melek Mikhael, and he is Sheikh Abu Bakr. Thursday he created Melek Azrael, and he is Sajad-ad-Din. Friday he created Melek Shemnael, and he is Nasir-ad-Din. Saturday he created Melek Nurael, and he is Yadin (Fakhr-ad-Din). And he made Melek Ta'us ruler over all.

After this God made the form of the seven heavens, the earth, the sun, and the moon. But Fakhr-ad-Din created man and the animals, and birds and beasts. He put them all in pockets of cloth, and came out of the Pearl accompanied by the Angels. Then he shouted at the Pearl with a loud voice. Thereupon the White Pearl broke up into four pieces, and from its midst came out the water which became an ocean. The world was round, and was not divided. Then he created Gabriel and the image of the bird. He sent Gabriel to set the four corners. He also made a vessel and descended in it for thirty thousand years. After this he came and dwelt in Mount Lalish. Then he cried out at the world, and the sea became solidified and the land appeared, but it began to shake. At this time he commanded Gabriel to bring two pieces of the White Pearl; one he placed beneath the earth, the other stayed at the gate of heaven. He then placed in them the sun and the moon; and from the scattered pieces of the White Pearl he created the stars which he hung in heaven as ornaments. He also created fruit-bearing trees and plants and mountains for ornaments to the earth. He created the throne over the carpet. Then the Great God said: "O Angels, I will create Adam and Eve; and from the essence of Adam shall proceed Shehar ben Jebr, and of him a separate community shall appear upon the earth, that of Azazil, *i.e.*, that of Melek Ta'us, which is the sect of the Yezidis. Then he sent Sheikh 'Adi ben Musafir from the land of Syria, and he came (and dwelt in Mount) Lalish. Then the Lord came down to the Black Mountain. Shouting, he created thirty thousand Meleks, and divided them into three divisions. They worshiped him for forty thousand years, when he delivered them to Melek Ta'us who went up with them to heaven. At this time the Lord came down to the Holy Land (*al-Kuds*), and commanded Gabriel to bring earth from the four corners of the world, earth, air, fire, and water. He created it and put in it the spirit of his own power, and called it Adam.

Then he commanded Gabriel to escort Adam into Paradise, and to tell him that he could eat from all the trees but not of wheat. Here Adam remained for a hundred years. Thereupon, Melek Ta'us asked God how Adam could multiply and have descendants if he were forbidden to eat of the grain. God answered, "I have put the whole matter into thy hands." Thereupon Melek Ta'us visited Adam and said "Have you eaten of the grain?" He answered, "No, God forbade me." Melek Ta'us replied and said, "Eat of the grain and all shall go better with thee." Then Adam ate of the grain and immediately his belly was inflated. But Melek Ta'us drove him out of the garden, and leaving him, ascended into heaven. Now Adam was troubled because his belly was inflated, for he had no outlet. God therefore sent a bird to him which pecked at his anus and made an outlet, and Adam was relieved.

Now Gabriel was away from Adam for a hundred years. And Adam was sad and weeping. Then God commanded Gabriel to create Eve from under the left shoulder of Adam. Now it came to pass, after the creation of Eve and of all the animals, that Adam and Eve quarreled over the question whether the human race should be descended from him or her, for each wished to be the sole begetter of the race. This quarrel originated in their observation of the fact that among animals both the male and the female were factors in the production of their respective species. After a long discussion Adam and Eve agreed on this: each should cast his seed into a jar, close it, and seal it with his own seal, and wait for nine months. When they opened the jars at the completion of this period, they found in Adam's jar two children, male and female. Now from these two our sect, the Yezidis, are descended. In Eve's jar they found naught but rotten worms emitting a foul odor. And God caused nipples to grow for Adam that he might suckle the children that proceeded from his jar. This is the reason why man has nipples.

After this Adam knew Eve, and she bore two children, male and female; and from these the Jews, the Christians, the Moslems, and other nations and sects are descended. But our first fathers are Seth, Noah, and Enosh, the righteous ones, who were descended from Adam only.

It came to pass that trouble arose between a man and his wife, resulting from the denial on the part of the woman that the man was her husband. The man persisted in his claim that she was his wife. The trouble between the two was settled, however, through one of the righteous men of our sect, who decreed that at every wedding a drum and a pipe should be played as a testimony to the fact that such a man and such a woman were married legally.

Then Melek Ta'us came down to earth for our sect (*i. e.*, the Yezidis), the created ones, and appointed kings for us, besides the kings of ancient Assyria, Nisroch, who is Nasir-ad-Din; Kamush, who is Melek Fakhr-ad-Din, and Artamis, who is Melek Shams-ad-Din. After this we had two kings, Shabur (Sapor) First (224-272 A. D.) and Second (309-379), who reigned one hundred and fifty years; and our amirs down to the present day have been descended from their seed. But we hated four kings.

Before Christ came into this world our religion was paganism. King Ahab was from among us. And the god of Ahab was called Beelzebub. Nowadays we call him Pir Bub. We had a king in Babylon, whose name was Bakhtnasar; another in Persia, whose name was Ahshurash; and still another in Constantinople, whose name was Agrikalus. The Jews, the Christians, the Moslems, and even the Persians, fought us; but they failed to subdue us, for in the strength of the Lord we prevailed against them. He teaches us the first and last science. And one of his teachings is:

Before heaven and earth existed, God was on the sea, as we formerly wrote you. He made himself a vessel and traveled in it in *kunsiniyat* of the seas, thus enjoying himself in himself. He then created the White Pearl and ruled over it for forty years. Afterward, growing angry at the Pearl, he kicked it; and it was a great surprise to see the mountains formed out of its cry; the hills out of its wonders; the heavens out of its smoke. Then God ascended to heaven, solidified it, established it without pillars. He then spat upon the ground, and taking a pen in hand, began to write a narrative of all the creation.

In the beginning he created six gods from himself and from his light, and their creation was as one lights a light from another light. And God said, "Now I have created the heavens; let some one of you go up and create something therein." Thereupon the second god ascended and created the sun; the third, the moon; the fourth, the vault of heaven; the fifth, the *farg* (i. e., the morning star); the sixth, paradise; the seventh, hell. We have already told you that after this they created Adam and Eve.

And know that besides the flood of Noah, there was another flood in this world. Now our sect, the Yezidis, are descended from Na'umi, an honored person, king of peace. We call him Melek Miran. The other sects are descended from Ham, who despised his father. The ship rested at a village called 'Ain Sifni, distant from Mosul about five parasangs. The cause of the first flood was the mockery of those who were without, Jews, Christians, Moslems, and others descended from Adam and Eve. We, on the other hand, are descended from Adam only, as already indicated. This second flood came upon our sect, the Yezidis. As the water rose and the ship floated, it came above Mount Sinjar, where it ran aground and was pierced by a rock. The serpent twisted itself like a cake and stopped the hole. Then the ship moved on and rested on Mount Judie.

Now the species of the serpent increased, and began to bite man and animal. It was finally caught and burned, and from its ashes fleas were created. From the time of the flood until now are seven thousand years. In every thousand years one of the seven gods descends to establish rules, statutes, and laws, after which he returns to his abode. While below, he sojourns with us, for we have every kind of holy places. This last time the god dwelt among us longer than any of the other gods who came before him. He confirmed the saints. He spoke in the Kurdish language. He also illuminated Mohammed, the prophet of the Ishmaelites, who had a servant named Mu'awiya. When God saw that Mohammed was not upright before him, he afflicted him with a headache. The prophet then asked his servant to shave his head, for Mu'awiya knew how to shave. He shaved his master in haste, and with some difficulty. As a result, he cut his head and made it bleed. Fearing that the blood might drop to the ground, Mu'awiya licked it with his tongue. Whereupon Mohammed asked, "What are you doing, Mu'awiya?" He replied, "I licked thy blood with my tongue, for I feared that it might drop to the ground." Then Mohammed said to him, "You have sinned, O Mu'awiya, you shall draw a nation after you. You shall oppose my sect." Mu'awiya answered and said, "Then I will not enter the world; I will not marry."

It came to pass that after some time God sent scorpions upon Mu'awiya, which bit him, causing his face to break out with poison. Physicians urged him to marry lest he die. Hearing this, he consented. They brought him an old woman, eighty years of age, in order that no child might be born. Mu'awiya knew his wife, and in the morning she appeared a woman of twenty-five, by the power of the great God. And she conceived and bore our god Yezid. But the foreign sects, ignorant of this fact, say that our god came from heaven, despised and driven out by the great God. For this reason they blaspheme him. In this they have erred. But we, the Yezidi sect, believe this not, for we know that he is one of the above-mentioned seven gods. We know the form of his person and his image. It is the form of a cock which we possess. None of us is allowed to utter his name, nor anything that resembles it, such as *Sheitan* (Satan), *kaitan* (cord), *shar* (evil), *shat* (river), and the like. Nor do we pronounce *mal'un* (accursed), or *la'anat* (curse), or *na'al* (horseshoe), or any word that has a similar sound. All these are forbidden us out of respect for him. So *khass* (lettuce) is debarred. We do not eat it, for it sounds like the name of our prophetess Khassiah. Fish is prohibited, in honor of Jonah the prophet. Likewise deer, for deer are the sheep of one of our prophets. The peacock is forbidden to our Sheikh and his disciples, for the sake of our Ta'us. Squash also is debarred. It is forbidden to pass water while standing, or to dress up while sitting down, or to go to the toilet room, or to take a bath according to the custom of the people. Whosoever does contrary to this is an infidel. Now the other sects, Jews, Christians, Moslems, and others, know not these things, because they dislike Melek Ta'us. He, therefore, does not teach them, nor does he visit them. But he dwelt among us; he delivered to us the doctrines, the rules, and the traditions, all of which have become an inheritance, handed down from father to son. After this, Melek Ta'us returned to heaven.

One of the seven gods made the *sanjaks* (standards) and gave them to Solomon the wise. After his death our kings received them. And when our god, the barbarian Yezid, was born, he received these *sanjaks* with great reverence, and bestowed them upon our sect. Moreover, he composed two songs in the Kurdish language to be sung before the *sanjkas* in this language, which is the most ancient and acceptable one. The meaning of the song is this:

Hallelujah to the jealous God.

As they sing it, they march before the *sanjaks* with timbrels and pipes. These *sanjaks* remain with our emir, who sits on the throne of Yezid. When these are sent away, the *kawwals* assemble with the emir, and the great general, the sheikh, who is the representative of Sheikh Nasir-ad-Din, *i. e.*, Nisroch, god of the ancient Assyrians. They visit the *sanjaks*. Then they send each *sanjak* in care of a *kawwal* to its own place; one to Halataneye, one to Aleppo, one to Russia, and one to Sinjar. These *sanjaks* art given to four *kawwals* by contract. Before they are sent, they are brought to Sheikh 'Adi's tomb, where they are baptized amid great singing and dancing. After this each of the contractors takes a load of dust from Sheikh 'Adi's tomb. He fashions it into small balls, each about the size of a gall nut, and carries them along with the *sanjaks* to give them away as blessings. When he approaches a town, he sends a crier before him to prepare the people to accept the *kawwal* and his *sanjak* with respect and honor. All turn out in fine clothes, carrying incense. The women shout, and all together sing joyful songs. The *kawwal* is entertained by the people with whom he stops. The rest give him silver presents, everyone according to his means.

Besides these four *sanjaks*, there are three others, seven in all. These three are kept in a sacred place for purposes of healing. Two of them, however, remain with Sheikh 'Adi, and the third remains in the village of Bahazanie, which is distant from Mosul about four hours. Every four months these *kawwals* travel about. One of them must travel in the province of the emir. They travel in a fixed order, differing each year. Every time he goes out, the traveler must cleanse himself with water made sour with *summak* (sumac) and anoint himself with an oil. He must also light a lamp at each idol that has a chamber. This is the law that pertains to the *sanjaks*.

The first day of our new year is called the *Sersalie, i. e.*, the beginning of a year. It falls on the Wednesday of the first week in April On that day there must be meat in every family. The wealthy must slaughter a lamb or an ox; the poor must kill a chicken or something else. These should be cooked on the night, the morning of which is Wednesday, New Year's day. With the break of day the food should be blessed. On the first day of the year alms should be given at tombs where the souls of the dead lie.

Now the girls, large and small, are to gather from the fields flowers of every kind that have a reddish color. They are to make them into bundles, and, after keeping them three days, they are to hang them on the doors as a sign of the baptism of the people living in the houses. In the morning all doors will be seen well decorated with red lilies. But women are to feed the poor and needy who pass by and have no food; this is to be done at the graves. But as to the *kawwals*, they are to go around the tombs with timbrels, singing in the Kurdish language. For so doing they are entitled to money. On the above-mentioned day of *Sersalie* no instruments of joy are to be played, because God is sitting on the throne (arranging decrees for the year), and commanding all the wise and the neighbors to come to him. And when he tells them that he will come down to earth with song and praise, all arise and rejoice before him and throw upon each the squash of the feast. Then God seals them with his own seal. And the great God gives a sealed decision to the god who is to come down. He, moreover, grants him power to do all things according to his own will. God prefers doing good and charity to fasting and praying. The worship of any idol, such as Seyed-ad-Din or Sheikh Shams is better than fasting. Some layman is to give a banquet to a *kochak* after the fasting of the latter forty days, whether it be in summer or in winter. If he (the *kochak*) says this entertainment is an alms given to the *sanjak*, then he is not released from his fasting. When it comes to pass that the yearly tithe-gatherer finds that the people have not fully paid their tithes, he whips them till they become sick, and some even die. The people are to give the *kochaks* money to fight the Roman army, and thus save the sect (Yezidis) from the wrath of the man of the year.

Every Friday a load of gifts is to be brought as an offering to an idol. At that time, a servant is to call the people aloud from the roof of a *kochak's* house, saying, it is the call of the prophet to a feast. All are to listen reverently and respectfully; and, on hearing it, every one is to kiss the ground and the stone on which he happens to lean.

It is our law that no *kawwal* shall pass a razor over his face. Our law regarding marriage is that at the time of the wedding a loaf of bread shall be taken from the house of a *kochak* and be divided between the bride and the bridegroom, each to eat one-half. They may, however, eat some dust from Sheikh 'Adi's tomb instead of the bread for a blessing. Marriage in the month of April is forbidden, for it is the first month of the year. This rule, however, does not apply to *kawwals*; they may marry during this month. No layman is allowed to marry a *kochak's* daughter. Everyone is to take a wife from his own class. But our emir may have for a wife any one whom he pleases to love. A layman may marry between the ages of ten and eighty; he may take for a wife one woman after another for a period of one year. On her way to the house of the bridegroom, a bride must visit the shrine of every idol she may happen to pass; even if she pass a Christian church, she must do the same. On her arrival at the bridegroom's house, he must hit her with a small stone in token of the fact that she must be under his authority. Moreover, a loaf of bread must be broken over her head as a sign to her that she must love the poor and needy. No Yezidi may sleep with his wife on the night the morning of which is Wednesday, and the night the morning of which is Friday. Whosoever does contrary to this commandment is an infidel. If a man steal the wife of his neighbor, or his own former wife, or her sister or mother, he is not obliged to give her dowry, for she is the booty of his hand. Daughters may not inherit their father's wealth. A young lady may be sold as an acre of land is sold. If she refuses to be married, then she must redeem herself by paying her father a sum of money earned by her service and the labor of her hand.

Here ends Kitab Resh.

اي كتاب الاسود

في البداية الله خلق درة البيضة من سرهِ العزيز وخلق طير اسمهُ انفر وجعل الدرة فوق ظهرهِ وسكن عليها اربعين الف سنة.

اول يوم الاحد خلق ملك عزازئيل وهـو طاوس مـلـك رئس الجميع.

يوم الاثنين خلق ملك درداثيل وهو الشيخ حسن.

يوم الثلاثا خلق ملك اسرافيل وهو شيخ شمس [الدين].

يوم الاربعا خلق ملك ميكائيل وهو شيخ ابو بكر.

يوم الخميس خلق ملك عزرائيل وهو سجادين.

يوم الجمعة خلق ملك شمنائيل وهو ناصر الدين

يوم السبت خلق ملك نورائيل وهو يدين [فخرالدين]

وجعل رئسًا على الجميع طاوس ملك. بعدما خلق صورة السبع سموات والارض والشمس والقمر وفخر الدين الانس والحيوان والطيور والوحوش ووضعهم في جبوب الخرقة وطلع من الدرة ومعه ملايكة فصاح على الدرة صيحة عظيمة فانفصلت وصارت اربعة قطع من بطنها خرج الماء وصار بحرًا وكانت الدنيا مدورة بـلا فراق ثـم خلق جبرائيل وصورة الطير وارسل بيدهِ ووضع اربع قرانى ثم خلق مركب ونزل فيهِ ثلاثين الف سنة. وبعد جاء وسكـن في جـبـل لالش وصاح في الدنيا مجمّد البحر وصارت ارض فبقت تهتز. فعند ذلك امر جبرائيل محاب قطعتيَن من الدرة البيضة فوضع واحدة تحت الارض وفي باب السماء سكنت الاخرى. ثم جعل فيهم شمس وقمر. وخلق النجوم من نثر الدرة البيضة وعلقهم في السـمـاء لاجل الزينة وخلق اشجار مثمرة ونباتات وجبال لاجل زينة الارض.

خلق عرش على الفرش. وقال الرب العظيم يا ملائكة انا اخلق آدم وحوا واجعلهم بشر ويكون من سر ادم شهر بن جبر. وايضًا منهُ يكون ملَّة على الارض تسمَّى ملة عزازئيل اعني طاوس ملك وهي ملة يزيدية. ثم ارسل شيخ عادي بن مسافر من ارض الشام فاتى الى لالش ثم نزل الرب الى جبل الاسود* وصاح وخلق ثلاثون الف ملك وفرقهم ثلاثة فرق وبدوا يعبدوا اربعون السف سنة ثم سلمهم الى طاوس ملك فصعد بهم الى السموات. ثم نزل الرب الى ارض القدس وامر جبرائيل فجاب تراب من اربع زوايا الارض تراب وهواء ونار وماء. فخلقهُ وجعل فيهِ روحًا من قدرتهِ وسماهُ آدم.

وامر جبرائيل ان يدخل ادم الى الفردوس ويامرهُ ان ياكل من كل الشجر فقط حنطة لا ياكل.

ثم بقى ماية سنة فقال طاوس ملك لله كيف يكثر ادم واين نسلهُ ان لم ياكل من شجرة الحنطة. قال لهُ الله الامر والتدبير سلمتهُ بيدك فجاء طاوس ملك وقال لادم اكلت حنطة فقال ادم لا لان الله نهاني. فقال طاوس ملك كل حنطة حتى يصير لك احسن. فاكل ادم من الحنطة وحالاً انتفخت بطنهُ فاخرجهُ طاوس ملك من الجنة وتركهُ وصعد الى السماء.

فتضايف آدم من نفح بطنه لانهُ ليس لهُ مخرج فارسل الله لهُ طيراً حتى جاء ونقرهُ وفتح لهُ مخرج فاستراح. وغاب عنهُ جبرائيل مائية سنة وادم حزين باكي.

فامر الله جبائيل ان يخلق حواء من تحت اباط الايسر. وبعدما خلقت حواء وكل الحيوانات تخاصما ادم وحواء على تناسل

67

الجنس البشري وكل واحد منهما يقول للاخر مـنـي هـو التناسل
وذلك لما نظروا شركة الذكر والانثى ما بـيـن الحيوانات وبعد
المباحثة بينهما صار الاتفاق على هذا وهو كل واحد القى شهوتهُ
بجرة وسدَّ فمها بختمه وصبروا تسعة اشهر وبعد ذلك فتحوها فنظروا
واذا بجرة آدم زوج صبيان ذكرًا وانثى ومـن هولاء تناسلت امتنا
ولما فَتحَت جرة حواء نَظر فيها دود معفَّنة مكروهة الراحة. وانبع
الله لادم ثدي وارضع الصبيان الذين خرجوا من جرتهِ. ولاجل
هذه المادة صار للرجل ثدي.

ومن بعد هذا عرف آدم حواء فولدَت ولديـن ذكرًا وانثى وهم
الذين منهم تناسلوا اليهود والنصارى والاسلام وغير ذلك مـن
الطوايف. اما شيث ونوح وانوش اناس ابرار وهم ابهاتنا الاولـيـن
ومن آدم فقط تناسلوا. وبعد هذا وقع خصومة بين رجل وامرأتهُ
بذلك الزمان الرجل يقول انها امرأتي والمرأة تقول ليس هو زوجي
نحكم بينهم واحد من امتنا الابرار وامر بان يكون بـكـل عرس
طبل وزرنايي وذلك لاجل الشهادة على الزواج لكيما يسمعون الناس
ان فلان اخذ فلانة ناموسيًّا

ثم نزل طاوس ملك الى الارض لاجـل طائفتنا الخلوقـة واقام
لنا ملوك. ما عدى ملوك الاثوريين القدماء. وهم نـسـروخ وهو
ناصردين وكاموش وهو ملك نخردين. وارطيموس وهو ملك شمس
دين. وبعد ذلك صار لنا ملكان شابور اول وثاني. ودام ملكهم
ماية وخمسون سنة ومن نسلهم اقاموا امرائنا الى الان. وبعضنا
اربعة ملوك. وكان قبل مجي المسيح الى هذا العالم تسمَّى ديانتنا
وثنية وكان ملك احاب مننا وكان يسمون اله احاب بعلزبول والان

عندنا يسمونه پيربوب. وكان لـنـا ملك في بابل اسـمـهُ بختنصر. واخر في الجم اسمهُ احشوراش. وفي القسطنطينيَّة ملك اخـر اسمهُ اغريقالوس. وكل اليهود والنصارى والاسلام وغير ذلك من الطوائف حتى الجم ايضاً قاوموا ديانتنا ولكن لا يقدروا علينا لان الهنا يقوينا عليهم ويعلمنا علم الاول والاخر ومن تعاليمه. انهُ قـبـل كون السماء والارض كان الله موجودًا على الإبحار [كما كتبنا لكم سابقاً] وانهُ صنع لهُ مركب يسير في كونسنيات الإبحار منترهاً في ذاته وانهُ خلق درة وحكم عليها اربعين سنة. ومـن بعد ذلك غـضـب عـلى الدرة فرفسها. فَيَا للجب الجيب ان صارت مـن فجيجيها الجبال ومن محيبيها التلال ومن دخانها السموات. فصعد الله الى السموات وجمّدها وثبّتها بغير عواميد وقفل عـلى الارض واخـذ قلم بيدهِ وبدى يكتب الخليقة كلها. ففي البداية خلق ستة الهة من ذاتهِ ومن نورهِ وهكذا خلْقتهم كانت تشبه انسان اذا اوقد سراج من سراج اخر.

فقال الله انا خلقت السماء فليصعد واحد مـنـكـم وليخلف شيأً فيها فصعد الثاني وخلق الشمس وصعد الثالث وخلق القمر والرابع خلق الفلك والخامس خلق الفرغ اي نجمة الصبح والسادس خلق الفردوس والسابع خلق جهنم. وبعد ذلك خلق آدم وحواء كما كتبنا لكم سابقاً.

واعلموا ان الطوفان الذي صار وقت نـوح صار طـوفـان آخـر بهذا العالم. وامتنا اليزيديَّة تناسلت مـن نعمي[31] لوجه[32] الملك

المكرم للسلام الذي يُدعَى عندنا ملك ميران . وباقي الطوايف
تناسلوا من حام الذي اهان ابيهِ .

اما السفينة فقامت في قريه عيـن سفنى تبعد عـن الموصل
خمسة فراسخ . وسبب الطوفان الاول هو من اجل استهزا الجـنس
البشري الخارجي كاليهود والنصارى والاسـلـلام وغـيـرهم الـذيـن
تناسلوا من ادم وحواء لا مثلنا نحن الذين تناسلنا مـن آدم
فقط كما عرفناكم . اما الطوفان الثاني نجاء على امتنا اليزيدية
ايضاً . فلما تعالت المياه وطافت السفينة فوق المآء صارت فـوق
جبل سنجار فصدمت بحجر فنقبت فتكعوكت الحية وسدت الثقب
فمضت السفينة واتكت على جبل جودي . فكثر جنس الحيَّة وكان
يلدغ الناس والحيوانات فامسكوها واحرقوها بالنار . فمن رمادها
صارت البراغيث في العالم .

ومن الطوفان الى الان سبعة الاف سنة . وبكل الف سنة ينزل
الاهًا واحدًا من السبعة آلهة يصنع لنا ايات وقوانين وشرايع ثم
يصعد الى مكانهِ . نزوله يصير عندنا لان جميع المكانات المقدسة
هي عندنا . وفي هذا الزمان نزل الله عندنا اكثر مـن الزمان
الماضي وثبَّت لنا الاولياء . وكان يكلمنا بلسان الكردي .

راضى على محمد نبي الاسماعيليين . وكان عند محـمـد خادم
اسمهُ معاويه . فنظر الله الى محـمـد انه لا يسلك مستقيمًا امامهُ
فاوجع راسهُ . فقال محـمـد لمعاويه تعال احلق راسي لانـهُ كان
يعرف يحلق فاتى معاويه وحلقهُ بخفةٍ وصعوبة حتى جرحهُ وجرى

70

منهُ دمًا. فلما نظر معاويه ذلك لسح الدم بلسانهِ خـوفًا لـئـلا يقع على الارض فقال لهُ محمد ماذا صنعت يا مـعـاويـه. اجـاب لحتهُ بلساني خوفي لئلا يقع دمك على الارض. فقال لهُ محـمد اخطيتَ بذلك يا معاويه انك ستجلب امة واحدة وراكَ" وتلقب[35] لامتي. فقال معاويه لا ادخل العالم واتزوج ابدًا. فـبـعـد زمان سلّط الله على معاويه عقارب فلدغتهُ ورشّ سمهم بوجههِ. فجزموا الاطباء ان يتنزوج وإلّ فيموت. فلما سـمـع ذلك رضيَ بـالزواج. نجابوا لهُ امرأة عجوز عمرها ثمانين سـنـة كي لا تحبل فعرفها وفي الغد ظهرت ابنت خمسة وعشرون سنة وذلك بقدرة الاله الكبير. نحبلت وولدت لالهنا الذي يدعى يزيد[36]. اما الامم الغريبة الذين ما يعرفون هذا يجدفون عليهِ. فقط غـلـطـوا بذلك وضلوا. اما عندنا نحن طائفة اليزيديّة لا نقبل ذلك لانـنـا نعرفهُ انـهُ هـو واحد من السبعة الالهة المذكورة. ونحن نـعـرف صورة شخصهِ وتمثالهِ وهي صورة الديك الذي عندنا ولا يجـوز لاحـد مننا ان يلفظ اسمهُ او يشابه اسمهُ كالشيطان وقيطان وشر وشط وما يشابه ذلك ولا لفظة ملعون او لعنة او نـعـل وما يشابه ذلك جميعها حرام علينا اولاً ثم احترامًا لهُ. ثم حرام علينا اكل الخس لانهُ على اسم نبيتنا الحاسيّة. والسـمـك علينا حرام احترامًا ليونان النبي. والغزال لانهُ غنم احـد انبيائنا. والشيخ وتلامذتهُ حـرام عليهم اكل الديك لطاوس الهنا والقرع ايضًا ما ياكلوهُ هولاء المذكورين. وحـرام البول وقوفًا. ولبس اللباس قعودًا. والاستخلاء

71

في مكان مخصوص كالعادة البلاد وغسل الحمام جميع ذلك حرام ومن خالفهُ فقد كفر. اما بقية الطوايف كاليهود والنصارى والاسلام وغير ذلك من الملل ما يعرفون هذه الاشياء لانهم ما يحبون طاوس ملك ولاجل هذا هو ايضًا ما يعلمهم ولا ينزل عندهم اما نحن معشر اليزيدية فاتى عندنا واسلم لنا الحقايف والايات والقوانين والتسلسومات حتى صارت كلها بالتناسل وراثة من الوالد الى الولد. ثم صعد الى السماء.

اما السناجق فان واحدًا من السبعة الالهة صنعهم واعطاهم الى سليمان الحكيم وبعد موت سليمان تسلموهم ملوكنا ويوم الذي ولد الهنا يزيد البربري[1] اخذ السناجق لامتا بتبجيل عظيم وصنع لهم مديحتيَن حتى يرتّلون بها ويزيّحون قدامهم بلسان الكردي المقبول والقديم [ومعنا الترتيل هو هذا هللوا لاله الغيور] والطبول والدفوف والشبابات قدامهم وموضع اقامة السناجق هو عند اميرنا الجالس على كرسي يزيد اما في ارسالهم يجتمعون القوالين عند الامير والشيخ الكبير العمومي ووكيل عوض الشيخ نصر الدين اي نسروخ الـه الاثوريين القدماء ويصفون بينهم افتقادًا على السناجق. ثم يرسلون الواحد الى الكلتيين والثاني الى حلب والثالث الى بلاد المسقوف والرابع الى جبل سنجار. هولاء الاربعة سناجق يعطون لهولاي القوالين بالضمانة. اولاً يمضون بهم الى الشيخ عادي هناك يعمدوهم بترتيل ورقص عظيم وياخذ كل واحد من هولاء المضمنين حملاً من تراب الشيخ عادي ويعملوهُ

بنادق بقدر العفص ويحملوهُ معهم مع السناجق حتى يعطوهُ
للبركة ولما يقترب صاحب السنجق لمدينة او الى قـريـة يـرسـل
قدامهُ منادي حتى يستعدوا لقبولهِ بالاكرام والتبجيل فيخرجون
جميعهم للغائة بثياب العز الفاخرة مع بخور وعـطـور والـنـسـاء
بالتهليل ويزمرون اية الفرح وعند دخولهِ تكون مزايدة العشر في
بيت الذي يحل فيهِ. اما بقية اهل البلد او القرية فيقدمون لهُ
هدايه فضة كل واحد على قدر لياقتهِ.

اما السناجق الثلاثة الذين بقوا مـن السبعة فبعد اخـراج
الاربعة المار ذكرهم يحفظون هولاء بمكان مقدس للشفاء اثـنـيـن
منهم يبقون بشيح عادي. والاخر بقرية بخزاني وهي عن الموصل
اربع ساعات. وكل اربعة اشهر يدوررون واحد منهم بولاية الامير.
وكل سنة واحد يدور وذلك بترتيب. وقبل الخروج يجب ان يغسل
بماء حمص بالسماق حتى ينظف مـن صدائهِ ثم يدهن بزيت.
ثم يوقد عند كل صنم عندهُ جرة سراجًا وهكـذا تـكـون امر
السناجق.

اما راس السنة عندنا فهو شهر نيسان ويوم الاربـعـا في اول
الاسبوع منهُ هو ليلة السرصالي [اعني راس السنة] كل بيت يجب
ان يوجد بهِ لحم الاغنباء يذبحون غنمًا او ثيران. والفقراء يذبحون
دجاجًا او غير ذلك. ويجب طبخهم ليلة الاربعا المذكورة وعـنـد
الفجر يباركون للاطعمة. وفي راس السـنـة يجـب الصـدقـة عند
انفس الموتى.

73

اما الشابات والبنات فعليهم ان يجمعوا مــن الــبــراري الورود والزهور من كل جنس ما كان لونهُ احمر ويشدوهُ باقات ويحفظوهُ ثلاثة ايام" ويضعوهُ بالابواب معمودية للبيت ففي الغد جـمـيـع الابواب يتراون متزينين بالسوسنان الاحمر. امـا النساء فيضعنَّ اطعمة على القبور لعابري الطريق من الفقراء والمساكـين الذين ليس لـهـم اطعمة. وللقوالين ان يدوروا حــول القـبـور بالدفوف والترتيل بلغة الكردية ولهم ان ياخذوا دراهمًا عوض ذلك.

وفي هذا يوم السرصالي" المذكور لا يدق فيهِ الات الطرب لان الله جالس على الكرسي ويامر ان يجتمعوا اليهِ العارفين والقربـاء ويقول لهم اني مزمع ان انزل عـلى الارض بالتبجيل والـتـسـبيح حينئذٍ يقومون جميعهم ويفرحون قدام الله ويلقون قرع التعييد عليهم ويختم الله بختم ثم يعطي الله الكبير صكـاً للاله الذي ينزل على الارض ويسلم بيدهِ السلطان ان يصنع كل شي كارادتهِ. اما الصوم والصلوة ان الله لا يشابهم لـكـن يريد الخير وعمل الصدقة وان احد الاصنام مثد جمادين او شيخ شمس هو احسن من الصوم. وعند صيام احد الكوجك اربعين من الصَيف او من الشتاء يجـب ان يصنع لـهُ احد العلمانيين وليمة واذا قال هذه الصدقة سنحف فلان يبطل صومهُ.

لان رجل السنة [اعنى عشار تلك الـسـنـة] لما يـنـظـر ان صدقاتهم ناقصة يضربهم بضربات كالموت والامراض وغير ذلك. وعندما يحدث ذلك يجب ان يعطي الكواجك درام حتى يقاتلوا

الجنود الرومايينين لكي يردوا غضب رجل السنة عن الامة. ويجب كل جمعه ان يقدم حملًا واحدًا من الصدقات قربانًا للصنم ثم يعطي الخادم تنبيهًا من فوق سطح بـيـت الكوجك بصوت عالٍ قايلاً دعوة نبي [اعني وليمة فلان] وثم يجـب ان ينصتوا الجميع باهتمام وايجاب وكل واحد يقبل الارض والجمر المتكي عليها. وايضاً من قوانيننا ان القوالين لا يعبروا موسى على وجوههم. وفي وقت الزواج يجب ان يعطي رغيف خبز من بيت الشيخ وذلك العريس ياكل نصفُه والعروس تاكل نصف الاخر وهو كناموس للزواج. او عوضًا عن الخبز ياكلون قليل من تراب الشيخ عادي للبركة وفي شهر نيسان كـحـرّم الزواج لانهُ راس الـسـنـة سوى الكواجك ماذون لهم ذلك. واما بنات الكواجك فليس للعلمانيين ياخذُم الاكل واحد ياخذ مـن جنسه. اما الاميـر ماذون لهُ ان ياخذ كل من يشتهيها. اما العوام فماذون لهم الزواج من ابن عشرة سنين حتى الثمانين وياخذ واحده بعد واحده مـن النساء الى الستة وعندما ياتون بالعروس الى بيت العريس يلزم ان تفتقد كل شـقـصٌ [قايمات الاصنام] تـمـر بهِ بطريقها ولو مرَّت ببيعة النصارى ايضًا ملزومة بذلك وعند وصولها لبيت العريس يـلـزم ان يضربها العريس بجمر صغيرة حتـى تكون تحت سلطانه وان يكسرون رغيف خبز على راسها حتى تكون حبة للفقراء والمساكين. وليلة الاربعا والجمعة يمنع مـن المضجع معها وكل هذا لازم عـلـى كل يزيدي ان يحفظهُ ويصنعهُ. ومن خالف كفر.

واذا خطف احد امرأت رفيقه او امرأته الاولى او اخته او امه ليس ملزوم ان يعطي مهرها لانها كسب يده اما البنات ليس لهم وراثة في بيت ابيهنَّ انما البنت تباع كالحقل وان أبـت عــن الزواج فيجب عليها ان توفي اباها بالخدمة وتعب يديها حـتـى يعتقها.

Printed in Great Britain
by Amazon